Daniel Kane

Ostentation of Peacocks

egg box

Ostentation of Peacocks

First Published, 2008, by Egg Box Publishing
www.eggboxpublishing.com

All rights reserved © Daniel Kane, 2008

The right of Daniel Kane
to be identified as the author of this work
has been asserted in accordance with Section 77
of the Copyright, Designs and Patents Act, 1988

This book is sold subject to the condition that it shall not,
by way of trade or otherwise, be lent, resold, hired out, stored in a
retrieval system, or otherwise circulated without the publisher's prior
consent in any form of binding or cover other than that in which it is
published and without a similar condition including this condition
being imposed on the subsequent purchaser.

Book Design:
Nathan Hamilton
& Anna Mae Selby

Cover & Interior Artwork:
Oliver Beavis

Printed and bound by:
Biddles, Kings Lynn
www.biddles.co.uk

ISBN: 978-0-954392-09-3

PRAISE FOR OSTENTATION OF PEACOCKS:

"Daniel Kane is the revitalising voice twenty-first century poetry needs, and *Ostentation of Peacocks* is a full display of his transatlantic talent. Fresh, funny and visionary, this book offers the reader a real world of fantasy with the lyric grace of early Ashbery and the prophetic ambition of early Ginsberg."

Jeremy Noel-Tod

"The funny thing about Daniel Kane's book, given its rather showy title, is how unostentatious his poems really are. Excessive, yes, gorgeously so; and 'out there' in bravely following his, or his given language's, inclinations. What is anything that can be observed or thought and how do our words account for, and even augment, that sketchy existence? How is a poem a fact if anything can be? Peculiar to Kane is his often headlong, always nimble variant on how to proceed: transmutation, an ostensible care for writing as fitting together a world in words as if out of nowhere. This remarkable book adds up, heartily, to its own 'heap big meal'."

Bill Berkson

"The variegated plumage of Kane's elegant, iridescent, fan-tailed poems is a constant delight. Some are indeed as ostentatious as peacocks in their pride, but others obliquely and movingly mime uncertainty, confusion, and loss. This is a gorgeous collection, and one that deserves a 'harmonious welcome'."

Mark Ford

PRAISE FOR OSTENTATION OF PEACOCKS:

"Fun is missing from this world everywhere; but here it is, at times pitiless but still fun. Daniel Kane's personable imagination dwells in the house of free play: a posture of meditation on the couch upon which there is ought to do but muse on things of a consequence neither relativized nor sanitized. Absolute inquiry into creatures-objects-ideas produces, in this leavened mind, a flurry of response that is a 'cosmos or order or harmony in a bag full of hard to categorize leaves'. Not only fun has been missing, but also compassion, and that is here too, 'with singular freshness and poignancy'."

Rebecca Wolff

"For all his talk about peacocks, cows, mares, turtles—his speaking to them, sometimes even flirting with them—Kane's repeated reminder that 'the material world is tenuous' suggests a deeper existential problem at the core of this excellent book. The natural world brims with life, sure, but the poet is still a bit anxious. Language itself hangs in the balance. The result is a book of poems with a New York School sensibility and a weirdly cuddly philosophical heart."

Aaron Belz

OSTENTATION OF PEACOCKS
by Daniel Kane

to Bubby

By The Same Author

All Poets Welcome: The Lower East Side Poetry Scene in the 1960s

What is Poetry: Conversations with the American Avant Garde

Don't Ever Get Famous: Essays on New York Writing After the New York School (editor and contributor)

CONTENTS

PART 1

OSTENTATION OF PEACOCKS	3
FISH 1 / FISH 2	4
BEGINNING WITH FLAPPING	6
BIRD AND LEAF COUPLETS	8
OSTENTATION OF PEACOCKS *continued*	9
SONNET	10
JEWISH VARIATIONS ON ERIK SATIE'S "SPORTS ET DIVERTISSEMENTS"	11
A DAIRY MAID IN THE ACT OF TEASING A COW THAT WISHES TO BE A DAIRY MAID	13
OSTENTATION OF PEACOCKS *continued*	14
LITTLE GOAT SONG	16
SUGGESTIONS	17
OSTENTATION OF PEACOCKS *continued*	18
THE WHOLE DARN LOT OF US	19
AMBIVALENT PICNIC	20
HOSTILE STUFF	21
VARIATIONS	22
OSTENTATION OF PEACOCKS *continued*	23

PART 2

SEVEN	27

PART 3

OSTENTATION OF PEACOCKS *continued*	37
SPIDER MELANCHOLIA	39
ABSENTEEISM IN THE WORK PLACE (FAT SONG)	41
OSTENTATION OF PEACOCKS *continued*	42
INVITATION	43
SONNET: DEAR FIRE	44
ALBATROSS SLAUGHTER	45
OSTENTATION OF PEACOCKS *continued*	46
2 ORNITHOLOGY VARIATIONS	47
POEM	48

CONTENTS

OSTENTATION OF PEACOCKS *continued*	49
I THOUGHT IT WOULD BE FUNNY	50
OSTENTATION OF PEACOCKS *continued*	51
KAYAK TRIP	53
OSTENTATION OF PEACOCKS *continued*	55
OSTENTATION OF PEACOCKS *continued*	57
I DID	59
SECOND DATE WITH ESTHER DRILL	60
OSTENTATION OF PEACOCKS *continued*	61
AGAINST FUN	62
OSTENTATION OF PEACOCKS *continued*	63
MUGOO	65
OSTENTATION OF PEACOCKS *continued*	66
POEM *the sexiness of the ancient world*	68
CHOCO-TACO CREAMY BURGER TINGLY CENTERS	69
OSTENTATION OF PEACOCKS *concluded*	70

PART 1

OSTENTATION OF PEACOCKS

A group of peacocks is called an ostentation of peacocks a muster of peacocks there is mustard and there is stuffing oh the beef we kill the cow to eat its meat I render a cloud a buzzard hornet whatever the sky knows what to do as long as I tell it to I say beef is in the oven here it comes served up smiling note harmonious welcome to my heap big meal.

FISH 1 / FISH 2

(for Alan and Naima)

FISH 1

Becalmed. Beware. The fish.
That's how they are all day.
Becalmed. Aware. The fish.
No fear of winter for the fish.

Spirits drifting no it's fish.
Bugle blow an answer for the fish.
Golden hours early spring / a pond.
March chill in air of watching drifting fish.

In dark trees there might be bracelets of the fish.
That there's seventeen poems no they're fish.
Another green world inside our darkest pond.
Fish here do survive this winter.

Toy ship brushing 'gainst the cheeks of fish.
Provoke St. Elmo's fire blossoms fish.
Come running up the hill through the sentence to the fish.
All in the same sense given would do here.

Fish here underhead this is the model.
Islands clouds and water heard again.
Surviving winter under layer one here ice.
Answer and you'll set the wild echoes flying

FISH 2

Becalmed. Beware. The fish.
That's how they are all day.
Becalmed. Aware. The fish.
No fear of winter for the fish.

Spirits drifting no it's fish.
Bugle blow an answer for the fish.
Golden hours early spring / a pond.
March chill in air of watching drifting fish.

In dark trees there might be bracelets of the fish.
That there's seventeen poems no they're fish.
Another green world inside our darkest pond.
Fish here do survive this winter.

Toy ship brushing 'gainst the cheeks of fish.
Provoke St. Elmo's fire blossoms fish.
Come running up the hill through the sentence to the fish.
All in the same sense given would do here.

Fish here underhead this is the model.
Islands clouds and water heard again.
Long stretches fish are the exception.
Answer and you'll set the wild echoes flying

A great fish of concentrated attention

BEGINNING WITH FLAPPING

The fly doesn't *flap* her wings she doesn't *flutter* them
what does she do what does the fly do what does the

hummingbird do for I have seen the hummingbird
suck from the bluebell or is it even bluebell and does the hummingbird

suck or sip does the fly flap or flutter and what does the pigeon
in his daily excursions do is he a flapper or a flyer

or a glider OK hawks glide of that I can be sure hawks glide
and seals flap their flippers on the rocks in the north west shores

of Scotland I do not cry out after the seal I do not wonder often
about the platypus as it sparkles in the waters of New Zealand

huh I saw a squirrel scamper and nibble and once a squirrel kind of
looked at me funny and then scampering and nibbling at the same time

scurried up a tree which was as far as I know in the process of
growing though it could have been dying as there was a mysterious

bulge in the tree a mysterious *bulge* as if some infection or tumor
had made its home in the trunk oh an ant just crossed my path I'll

slap it I'll slap it with my flip-flop and a duck just landed in the
swimming pool or does it land does it merely slide or settle

does it *settle* or *slide* or *land* into the pool a naked
man can be like a river a body can have a coastline a baby

can be a forest of blood and you can wear a wedding dress but
a cat never slouches a crane's neck bends and it doesn't so much

peck at the water as test it yes I'd say a crane tests the water
before consuming the fly and the fly doesn't flap her wings and

nibble and a squirrel kind of day or a crane day or ant moment
a million gray rats life and a platypus a breeze of coral and

life who would be like a river if life could be
like a river when that is the world at sunrise with a fly and ant and more

BIRD AND LEAF COUPLETS

I have yet to meet a vulture I didn't like.
A willow leaf can give sage advice but is sometimes prone to pedantry.

Swans are violent creatures. Never approach a swan for a loan.
Oak leaves nudge each other in the wind in much the same way oxen do.

A parrot is practically designed to entertain.
The larch produces a 'fun' kind of leaf.

Be careful to lube the sparrow up liberally before you fuck it in the ass.
A bay leaf once encouraged me to sidle up to Nancy.

I once heard there's a myth to the myna bird.
Rose leaf not petal not leaf.

A crass bird is the cockatoo.
The elm leaf is not to be trusted around children.

Ravening towards rest comes you guessed it the raven.
Apply the healing balm of the aloe vera leaf to your burn.

The crow has advised me to 'drop' Lytle as a friend.
The pine leaf whispers Bettina's secrets to me.

I immediately turn away from the attacking seagull.
A cosmos or order or harmony in a bag full of hard to categorize leaves?

OSTENTATION OF PEACOCKS *continued*

I've got a real pain in my stomach today it is the pain of sorrow this is my candid admission little butter cup little ladybird oh little fox terrier designed so cute is that you Hosanna don't make me blush I know I have terrifically gorgeous big brown eyes eyelashes that some people insist are made ostentatious through mascara do you like me.

YES I sniff airplane glue YES I am generally engorged with pleasure YES you are absolutely delightful have you prepared the meat plate and when is the weather actually going to happen what is now predicted has been predicted and will come true as has always been predicted a couple of long notes before the horrid claw gets through the gate.

Those things that are pretty include a little pot of peat or buzzard or bee well what else is there to say I haven't had a delicious plate of ribs in gosh I don't know how long I wonder what Aaron Belz is doing now is he fishing or is he watching TV every now and then getting up off his Christian ass to adjust the rabbit ears Aaron dig right in it's beef.

SONNET

Each multiplex movie carves a tale into the boy.
After many years the boy is a drooling idiot.
The boy's drool is the movie-mogul's guilt.
The boy is sent to bed.
The guilt gets a little anxious, then scrams
Looking for that sweet little number named Sue.
His insecurity hums.
It vibrates to distraction from the October tree
The last obdurate leaf.
Not surprisingly, anxious birds bleat like weird sheep.
There's no such thing as a forest, not really.
A movie lot, some actors, gaffers, a "boom."

Children, be the trees your sleep awaits.
Turn off your pen-lights, shut your million eyes.

JEWISH VARIATIONS ON ERIK SATIE'S "SPORTS ET DIVERTISSEMENTS"

THE BALANCER
It's my heart that balances like anise. It's got nothing to do
with vertigo. Come on and follow my little feet.

THE FISH
Murmurs of you in a light on the river. Venue
suitable for a fish. Or another fish.
Give me two fish.
"Do you have a pill?" "It's a fish, a poor
fish." Lord have mercy. "Jack returns cheese here,"
the fisherman mumbles. The Jews murmur
with their lights on the river.

THE BATH OFFICER
The sea may be large, madame, but it's all ours. In your house, you season
your big ass. No use assaying this dance of fronds

it's plain to the other Jews. "You are tooting
mussels!" "Yes, ma'am, I am."

THE CARNIVAL
The confetti descends. Voices and masks.
A Pierrot in the stage-set library catches a marlin.
Strictly not kosher.
Turn on the lights and bells, uh-huh.

THE POOR
The poor are inside a cavern. She is amused with

these crabs. She pursues them. She is availing and traversing.
Haggard, she marches on their heads. She bites a Jew
who reminds her of Demeter.

THE FOUR COINS
The four sewers. The Jewish chat. The sewer-agents the
chat. The chat entire. And the lance. The chat is well-placed.

THE PICNIC
"And for you are these three freezing Jews."
"Thanks. Why don't you lay your head on this lovely white church-robe?"
"Holy shit, an airplane!"
"No, no, hush, it's just an orange."

THE BAD FLIRTING
"How are you?" "No
Jew I've ever met is amiable." "Lash me!"
"You are like a gross Jew." "My voodoo
has entranced the moon." "Just as I suspected. I'll hock your tit."

THE ARTIFICIAL FOOL
Oh, a fool from Bengal!
A fusion! A completely blue fusion...

THE TENNIS
"Play?" "Yes!" The good servant. Come
and spread jam on these balls. There's a good servant. Service
me, please, service me... "Game!"

A DAIRY MAID IN THE ACT OF TEASING A COW THAT WISHES TO BE A DAIRY MAID

DAIRY MAID:

You'll never make a good dairy maid,
a novel, fresh, or even interesting specimen of a dairy maid,
a mere stray phenomenon of a dairy maid,
a single-minded, meek, or long suffering dairy maid,
a vibrant, humming, louvred belfry of a dairy maid,
a homely, hacking, disturbed clod of a dairy maid,
a miraculously white, warm and muggy dairy maid,
a leaden evening sky of a dairy maid.

COW:

Eugh! Eugh!

OSTENTATION OF PEACOCKS *continued*

Feed mixed grains game bird crumbles and a variety of greens to the Indian Blue the Black-shouldered one the White and the Pied and make sure to preheat the oven to two hundred degrees as we sing our song to the bird who hardly ever becomes sick remember the one peacock that lived to be forty years old remember his lofty spirit his eyes divine.

It's true I'm afraid of my own death OK fine so why are you still bothering me shall I extend the discussion of the realism shall we see in respect that everything is a kind of documentary show a clip provide us with snapshots of a vanishing age how things once were when monsters waltzed the earth what is there my lobelia my anus my big fat anus.

As Hosanna reported few peacock species are used for food except in the less civilized places where they are found in nature and when a tree wavers it does so not out of nervousness or insecurity but because the wind has rustled it would that our lives were so simple along the lines of the peafowl who naturally do not stray far from home.

The ferocity of the grizzly bear as it pounces on the peacock oh dear the peacock's being ripped to shreds by the bear cackle ACK ACK better idea to tear apart creepy K— E— or awful J— P— believe in hidden impulses embrace the bear within nurture the dwarf roast the ocelot undo the unbelievable lips drench the besotted American cod.

I am generally engorged with pleasure I enjoy a good steak I love ice-cream especially when it is free I tend to stay away from modified or processed food products though fizzy cola bottle gummies which some continue to insist is made out of horse gelatin still gives me heap big kicks hey the wind just rustled oh that it would forever can you make it so.

We love them most of the time though they make obnoxious mating calls a face can turn into a camel's face under the right conditions couples can resemble the dogs they own when we look out a window in a city during the night and see light past other people's windows well I'm sentimental the word 'tender' the word 'foreskin' a weeping stranger.

No surprise peacock beautiful to behold but to touch the peacock is only asking for trouble it would be best if we stuck to our neck of the woods and they stuck to theirs they can eat grain we can make grilled cheese sandwiches avoid flares of color while the games-keeper with his brush and pan sweeps the feathers off the tarmac of the manse.

LITTLE GOAT SONG

I took a journey first to see
my favorite goat inside the leaves
my wish to see what it had been
became my wish to sin and sin

Such strength in transformation comes
As tingles in the bones,

A nervous system's in the world,
a goat, a thrilling zone.

SUGGESTIONS

1.

The way is dark so set yourself
on fire make yourself a torch make

of yourself a torch in the distance
eternal amorous hilarity

there you'll be happy hey
you're almost there

lift your sightless
eyes I too drift coming near you

2.

The way is dark so set yourself
on fire make yourself a torch make

of yourself a torch in the distance
eternal amorous hilarity

there you might be happy hey
you're almost there

lift your sightless
eyes I drift coming near you

OSTENTATION OF PEACOCKS *continued*

He wanted her she wanted him they were very interested in taking each other's clothes off there is such a thing as desire which trembles with rhyme we are very interested in the basics we continue to be so like monastic restraint like blue pitcher full of water like wind in nostril like AAK yeah people enjoy polar bears they like seals barking ponies rolling.

Kathryn calls him The Hedgehog oh come on come on angrily the Monster is loose and has dragged the bird so far into the crummy forest that all hope is lost what about the inner eye and I ain't talking asshole mister for example the ontological argument of the moving picture with its great abilities the way a horror movie is for example Blood Feast.

Someone asked me why my interest in peacocks aren't we all interested don't we enjoy their insane cry don't we love going to the Bible Garden behind St. John the Divine to impress our date with the two peacocks who make their home there the swing set an old woman who waylays you asking what you read the occasional priest fierce with anger.

I enjoy the night sky just like a lot of folk do I love the way the wind makes a mysterious home in the night sky I love the flap of a wing I love the duck that roasts in my oven I love all my friends who love me for my love of roasting a variety of game and farm birds I used to love Dr. Pepper but now it's more about loving the night sky and some wind.

THE WHOLE DARN LOT OF US

Little Snip-Snaps called off her marriage engagement
and went to the local bar, where she drank seven
gin martinis with the editor of the "Paris Review."
She noticed his bald dome was offset nicely by his salt-and-pepper
beard as he spoke in the voices of the famous and not-so-famous
dead. Robert Browning used to do this too – as far as we know
he was "off his rocker." My Granny

        was also cuckoo, but now
her insanity is subsumed by senility. She wears seven festive jump-
suits a week as if preparing to parachute at a moment's
notice,which she'll do soon, as will you, and me,
and Little Snip-Snaps, all of us

making our various mortal noises
including the immortal "wheeeeee!!"

AMBIVALENT PICNIC

(after Joseph Ceravolo)

Mistook, no, wet
streets, until
not a pita-pocket you chime in
you love,
with axe. What will
you do to me when I grow up? I wait
for your face, who
are you and what are you
doing here? Would it
help you have me
do animal things and
sort some pie? Is appellation
important to you and if so
woof woof woof I am
a dog uncomfortable in a strange park
no leash or tags. The children call
you an ugly girl who cares I am not
at all influenced by their opinions.
Hide with me here under the shade
of this tree ugly girl and plumbs,
lie down and plumbs or thermos of two o'clock mistook
no, wet streets, until

HOSTILE STUFF

He almost shaved his ball-hair off
but decided against it. Instead, he chose to sit

on a porch constructed not out of wood
but out of sun shafts: it was like "a porch

of renovated time,"
but comfortable enough for his purposes.

What did he do once he sat there?

What do you *think*
he did   Asshole?

VARIATIONS

(after Flaubert)

1.

Strap on your new silver spurs at the mounting-block;
there's a new girl in town. Blow down

some bits of flower from your window;
there's a new girl in town. You're lonely,

you're lonely, but wipe off that frown;
a new girl in town   a new girl in town

2.

From your window blow down
to him some bit of flower or leaf
that you bit off in your teeth.

Don't be hesitant, embarrassed.
Be romantic, romantic.

3.

The old white mare is standing motionless
at the door   the old white mare motionless
near the door white mare motionless standing
at the door white mare old just standing there
barely moving near the door

4.

A tangled mane is hesitant a tangled
mane alone no horse attached to it
a tangled mane a tangled.

5.

Like a bird in the street a bit of flower flutters from the window
a bit of flower that he bit off in his teeth in the street that she
bit off in her teeth a bit of like a bird in the street.

6.

Weaving semicircles in the air the old white mare
stands less than motionless nowhere near the door
from your window blow down and strap on your silver
spurs from the mounting-block near the door blow down
standing there be there and/or talk to him
from above leaning out your window chewing
a bit of flower a bit of leaf.

7.

In the street, Charles would strap on his spurs at the mounting-
block; and she would continue to talk to him from above, blowing
down to him some bit of flower or leaf she had bitten off in her
teeth. It would flutter down hesitantly, weaving semicircles in the
air like a bird, and before reaching the ground it would catch in
the tangled mane of the old white mare standing motionless
at the door.

OSTENTATION OF PEACOCKS *continued*

A man said the turtle's poking its head out of the shell a man said I'm going to lay some cable a man said I'm going to pinch a loaf a man said I'm going to crop spray a man said I'm going to drop the kids off at the pool Lewis said withered vine Lewis said old tree Lewis said lean horse Lewis said sun there sky's edge oh again she said more she said.

PART 2

SEVEN

1.
There is a beginning there is a question what kinds of numbers are out there. One – unity sovereignty a rapt sheep on shore an expression a giggle followed by a single laugh then a drifting eyelash. One – as in an eyeball from which we see one thing a thong. We were in Fairfax Anselm Berrigan was there a motion passed a voter began weeping. I'm collecting mathematical definitions of numbers a palm tree a sandlot a kid with a cap with a pizza in the eye beneath one little forehead protecting a brain the best source of freedom outside of bubblegum. I mean it. Gazelles are fine but nothing compares to a solitary sheep standing on the edge of the Sussex shore. Oh plasma oh chips oh the lonely lettuce leaf the abandoned cat. I am lonely with this number though I guess this is as good as it gets. An ostrich backs up against a sheep. We share the planet with lots of living things which I urge you to think about at length. I am a spokesperson for all sentient beings I am magnificent.

2.
For the last two thousand years it has been this conception that is at the heart of our feeling about poetry. Two – that in the mouth of two witnesses the truth may be established. Cate Marvin sang two songs and hurt two men with them. Kafka no something less literary OK two prams. A lazy caterer forgets to include love in his recipe and the twins are left to hide their disappointment when faced with the bland birthday cake. A palindrome free in the square frightens the children out of their wits and two wigs are lost in the mayhem. Stan Ulam solved the problem of how to initiate fusion in the hydrogen bomb for which we are all graceful. The two voyagers are at the gate what shall we greet them with the ribbon of fire or the girdle of concrete. A couple of fun people with bright smiles and a sense of purpose as in Battlestar Galactica decide to hijack a train. The best time or I should say one of the best times I ever had with her was at the Torture Museum. First there was one now there are two rapt sheep. There were two guards looking like gorillas with him. I came with my wife.

3.
The world is not divided into two but is always conjoined in three. While buying Abba Zabbas at the supermarket Gregor was delighted to discover a three-for-one sale. Has there ever been anything as lyrical as Alice Notley singing three times. Three – stretch forth your body over a dead child three times and the child shall live again. Below are three sheep each in its way appearing rapt in meditation. Three wise men in love with Nancy Shapiro. The number three is overwhelming the prose. Guess what evil numbers are I won't tell you. What was my father doing walking up Christopher Street on July 9th 1999. Three times three is nine sorry to break it to you. Three sheep killed mumbled Sister Silbhe she was seldom the focus of so much attention. How much power. What is a joke number. Three sheep stood around looking at each other each one waiting for the other two to blink.

4.

It used to be there was the illusion of democracy but now we don't even have that to rely on. Aaron Belz wandered lonely as a cloud and he still does four days out of seven. Four – all points all directions everywhere a compass. We took a walk through the palace together and realized we were completely out of place. I invoke the powers invested in me by the number four but hey keep your tits on. As they paddled slowly down the Ganges four young osteopaths came to realize themselves as shining jewels of the universe along the lines of Brahmaputra. Measuring the world with his three strides he came upon something unspeakably horrible which forever altered the triad. Today four sheep showed up but refused to applaud. The fountain overflows and I am lost without you. Four ever sounds like forever which doesn't mean much beyond the page. Two and two make for sheep.

5.
For ever and ever and a hum oh rasps and hummock of a chosen day. Five flocks of sheep driven through the storm and there stands Sebastian with quiet eyes and rapt forehead. I heard Ange Mlinko had a baby which made it out alive – that's great! A prose velocity too fast for narrative or image-making. Five – flowers are picked up with the right hand and then the fingers are pointed downward so that the flowers fall at the feet of the god. Five fingers five senses. Dreaming in Catalan oh Barcelona the fountain five persimmons one bright day. Five civilians were accidentally killed when the military held a bake sale. Velocity crank damn little hotspur a moose five horns and a truck. It took them five days to sell off one man's possessions. I don't care what the white man say Santa Claus was a black man. Until one watches Fox News Channel Five nothing will be clear and then when one watches Fox News Channel Five everything is clarified and the flowers bloom. How many times do I have to tell you. Five rapt sheep aim themselves at eleven Xerox locations worldwide. Additional savings for military shoppers.

6.
I am getting sick of trying to temper my tantrums. It's true that it's very frustrating when the tortilla doesn't just slide out of the pan. I don't care about the number of the beast it's too predictable. Six – in six days work was complete and Larry Fagin invited us over for dinner. Who is the sky who is the universe who made the universe who wills the birds as the butterflies as the flowers which drop at the feet of the gods. Six sheep rapt on shore. A covenant was made with the children of Israel. She wondered if he really loved her. My other wife is a Cadillac. I came with my wife six times we loved it so much. Sheaf or sheep or sheer. They tried not to face the fact that they were being lied to by the men in power but after a while they realized they'd rather be fishing anyway. Votes count. Six days you shall labor. I lived in Mexico for six years and therefore compared to you I am exotic. Backstage at Radio City Music Hall past the Rockettes' dressing rooms three camels six sheep two donkeys and a horse keep a woman awake each night. Desire tremble your rhyme this is my hand your hand we are kissing in time.

7.
Assuming we're not counting the presence of a great sunbeam a large brook and not far from the church a wooden bridge there is no one listening to us. Running away from the elephant came a little man with a cowlick he barked seven times. Ginger was stupefied by the marvelous appearance of seven burning sheep on the Sussex shore. And I beheld in the midst of the throne in the midst of the elders stood a Sheep as it had been slain having seven horns seven eyes which are the seven spirits of God sent forth. As I told Lisa Jarnot I'm really lost hopelessly immersed in lyric. Seven angels seven steps seven planetary spheres. Seven mouths of the Ganges and the Nile seven dwarves. Seven parts of the body seventy paragraphs for a contract with the devil seven herbs for the magical drinks prepared with the help of the enemy of man. The seven sages the seven worlds the seven holy cities seven holy seas. Seven holy mountains the seven deserts seven sacred trees. The child is not held responsible for any crime till he is seven.

PART 3

OSTENTATION OF PEACOCKS *continued*

Dry lives a curtsying daisy scents filters and silks the lord of the rings the fellowship of the rings life on a string my girl Friday extremely large nipples the little foxes the cranes are flying a man with a rubber hand the truck Jenny's hand the truck in Boom Town Jenny and the Man with the Rubber Hand Jenny and the peacock the truck the truck.

Oh flap and insane cry I wonder why it is that none of the poets like me and by that I'm talking literally except for L except for A except for A except for T except for L except for L except for C though he is suspicious except for Betsy Bull I am too ostentatious I will take fire uh oh here comes creepy-crawly K— E—

The Fellowship is a bright island threatened by countless orcs in the surrounding darkness that is only ameliorated when the glorious peacock deigns to saunter forth with its bright plumage spread there is so much light emitted I love the way that the bird refuses this earthly life well the peacock bear in mind was once pillaged in this place.

Tomorrow there will be great delight as Hosanna shows everyone her hairy arms and bearded clam and popcorn will be made in which the pot that it is made in does not burn the flesh off the poor boy's wrist there are cultures where gaps are praised gat-toothed women are praised large gap Lauren Hutton exquisitely beautiful NOT A ROBOT.

Oh my peacock did you come here on a spaceship was the spaceship protected by a high-reflectance screen how did you get those blues and oranges is that orange we cannot move into the painted portions of your frame without seeming to disappear richer and warmer with orange and coral bright green and yellow spaceships blinking taking off.

Some of them wouldn't but you wouldn't want to be with them anyway oh what is mauve mother what is purple what is teal mother take love and root it into our hearts take it and root it for glorious bird that sings not from the tree but from the amusing bush or hedge calls forth great laughter and marzipan week after week day in day out yeah doggie style.

Mount a bird fuck it good lube it up yeah go nuts dart your tongue down the bird's throat then rub the bird on fallen snow drag the bird up to Earth's orison hire the sun as the bird's chariot spew on the wing pat bird cum on K— E— time your own cum in time for 'Jeopardy' creepy K— E— recounts bird rape in his blog cry oh boy heap scratchy lay.

SPIDER MELANCHOLIA

The spider got drowned
in the shower today.

The spider got drowned in the
shower today.

I was responsible
for drowning the spider.

I aimed my nozzle
full on at that spider.

I watched that spider
get carried away

on the stream I created
with my shower nozzle.

That spider it spasmed
as it got carried away

to the dismal drain
on the stream I created.

I feel awful 'bout this
and lots of other stuff too

like seeing friendless young Nick
picking at the cheese plate

or those mongoloids on the bus
hitting each other

how they laughed and brayed
like cartoon donkeys.

I sometimes dream
that I'll get killed

by a very large bus
by a bus or something.

ABSENTEEISM IN THE WORK PLACE (FAT SONG)

I'm cleaning like mad "Who did it and ran" is what they'll be thinking if they show up to find my house this pigsty as if I were never here

"Who did it and ran" I hope you're having a wonderful time this Labor Day weekend I can't come into work I'm making cheesecake for next weekend that's why no come into work tomorrow making cheesecake things like that

no LIKE THAT and I'm cleaning like mad "Who did it and ran" are you coming into work tomorrow I can't work not even next weekend can I might not be in tomorrow I might not be in for the rest of the week

and I'm making cheesecake and marinating beef for next weekend BEEF things like that making cheesecake and marinating BEEF things like that and I'm cleaning like mad "Who did it and ran" I said "Who did it and ran"

they might say and "Catch as catch can" they might say and I hope you're having a wonderful time I'm making cheesecake next weekend making cheesecake and marinating BEEF

BEEF things like that so I might not be in for the rest of my life like a ball of yarn next weekend I am yes like a ball of yarn and it is beautiful isn't it and it is beautiful isn't

it and marinating beef and making cheesecake is there it is delicious isn't it it is beautiful isn't it

OSTENTATION OF PEACOCKS *continued*

I am afraid of the one who is carrying the blade gleaming and sharp I am so gentle in comparison I sing hallelujah with reverent voice I drive the car divine and when the elder calls angels and peacocks in dance in life eternal I come whirling down happy basically I'm so much nicer than most people I know I cheerfully arise out of flesh into spirit.

We all woke up a little and ate some pepperoni and to the one that led us here waxing in beauty our tongues moved to speak and we urged him in whom power lay to save us from perdition to even perhaps help us develop some special moves for the peacock dance that we were working on and so he revived with what hymns and opened as a rose into violet.

And so a trumpet blew the air cold and we ran down the street and around the block in mad hope to find Ding-Dong Valley where we could be safe where angel music and whatnot and Indians without garbage would welcome us as into a heavenly realm sure we were scared but the blazing peacock eyes that illuminated our way sure helped I tell you.

Why worry about the Beast with pointed tail remember the beef's still in the oven we've got BEEF BEEF things like that ignore the horrid shaggy armpits and the stained noose hanging from the chandelier L's here that helps T with his hilarious manifold hatreds is here that's pretty great too and maybe Joe will show up and blow a trumpet.

Even as the ostentation of peacocks at the sound of the trumpet blast went flocking through the welkin with quicker wing than anyone thought possible another then appeared whose cheek grief distilled with water and we called to the gods as was our habit and asked her name for we wished to clasp her it's that old let me hold you impulse.

B – i – ngo B – i – ngo B – i – ngo and bingo were her name-o there was a farmer big fat fuck and cuntface fucking ass-flaps B – i – ngo B – i – ngo B – i – ngo and cuntface was her name-o there was a twat its sanguine flaps and bingo were her name-o B – i – ngo B – i – ngo B – i – ngo and bingo were her name o there was a cunt its snout so long and bing

INVITATION

There are times when your stomach 'problems' reconstruct your consciousness to the point that the local atmosphere takes on the shimmer of a foreign country you lived in long ago. Brooklyn

becomes Czechoslovakia, which itself no longer exists. Dear _____, you are invited to a party on Saturday, March 11, 3:30 p.m., at Pierrepont Playground. Do you think you can make it despite the fact that the very physicality of our environment appears tenuous? Do you

have anything to 'say'? The teaching industry seems to think so. They are convinced of the fantasy that everyone, if handed the right tools, has an equal right to express him or herself in a unique and fascinating way. This despite the facts. Look,

meet me at the playground at 3:30 for football, then walk with me to my house for a meal and cake.

SONNET: DEAR FIRE

I was very scared when I smelled your smoke
and sniffed about my apartment looking for you
and glimpsed your brutal dancing reflection on the metal sheen
       of the toaster-oven.

I was so happy that the reflection was coming from the outside
in the garden where the white people were making you
out of gasoline and strung-together bales of sticks.

For about ten seconds I thought I'd have to fight you with water
and perhaps 'die in the struggle'. My heart

is still pumping outrageously
from the fear you called up in me.

ALBATROSS SLAUGHTER

I am very sad that albatrosses' wings
are getting lopped off by European windmill
blades it's not like there's a glut of albatrosses

I was thinking the other day by the pond
that I know so little of what's going on on the surface
of the pond its lily pads or are they even lily pads

That said I have seen the albatrosses - which can have a wingspan
of up to eleven feet - while sailing in the southern oceans. The sight is one
      that I will never forget and I find it impossible to accept

      that the albatross might one day be lost for ever. Isn't anyone else
sad I mean come on isn't anyone else sad. I'm a little bird in the wilderness
all sad like dry glue on paper or a blind butterfly or some kind of weird *shape*

OSTENTATION OF PEACOCKS *continued*

The terrific grasshopper story your own experience whilst under the influence of drugs the prison trials the enormous tribe of ostrich the unbelievable sight of a valley full of ostriches the incredible vision of a gulf humming with peacocks anticipating objections to your argument your lovely brassiere persons people public a say person sitting on a lawn.

Note generic arguments about documentaries note ontological arguments note that in effect what is essentially documentary is laid over the top of the heart approach watch and talk a little bit let the pure visual effect of watching stuff approach the action of the movement of trees how does this allow us to approach other sorts of shows discuss a clip.

Place a sprig of daisy on the beef watch the evil trolls scamper no trolls allowed here sorry boys now with the white then with the yellow and then with the violet take the key unblock the passage let the girl banging on the door into the feast humbly request or devoutly fall in front of the Bird Divine and then oh do discover what it is she has to say.

My feelings for you run deeper than the highest mountain I love everything about you even the way you make me suicidal when you poopoo my ideas everywhere I go I think I see you Pams House Liquid Ponanas even School Daze at LCR I would have sworn I saw you at Primark the other day but when I called out you didn't reply I love it the most –

Not a refined or generous idea was ever born in this place never before have I entertained so low an idea of the beauty and perfection of man's nature never have I seen humanity in so degraded a shape as here ignorance vulgarity rudeness conceit and dullness are the reigning gods of this deuced sink of despair who said that Jeremy you sent it to me.

2 ORNITHOLOGY VARIATIONS

I.

It's O.K. that the material world is tenuous.
However, I must remind myself to 'grab it

by the shoulders' and 'give it a shake' in case
it gets cancelled entirely. If the phone rings,

I'll pick it up on the first chirp – why wait
for the second or the third? The desire to impress

in this way is depressing. Now is the time
to look out my window in case I miss the sparrow.

II.

I talk on the phone to Julie, who wants to meet
me tomorrow at 1:15. Imminence of lending a book,

owing a dollar. Will I make it until then?
When she called I picked the phone up on the first

ring. That gave her a little shock; the immediate
crackle of my voice. Julie, where does the grackle

live? is its plumage variegated?

POEM

Every bird and every leaf speaks to me.

Hello there says a little bird and hi! hi! says a little leaf.

What I wouldn't do for a good long conversation with a walrus but I am in the wrong hemisphere and anyway the walrus is no bird nor any leaf.

OSTENTATION OF PEACOCKS *continued*

Um boys you should know that in Hinduism the image of the god of thunder rains and war Indra was depicted in the form of a peacock in south India peacock is considered as a 'vahana' or vehicle of lord Muruga the figure of peacock is painted in various Islamic religious buildings in Christianity the peacock is known as symbol of the 'Resurrection'.

Like in India people believe that whenever the cock spread its tails in an ornamental fashion it indicates that rain is imminent in a way it is partly true at the sight of dark clouds the bird outspreads its tail and starts dancing in rhythmic fashion most of the folklore including Bharatha Natyam has got special dancing poses for the peacock dance.

Fat fuck cuntface fucking assflaps b – i – ngo and cuntface was her name-o scratching her butt her still banging on the door hoping admission she list colors we kiss big fat crane together we enjoy flying man with rubber hand the truck here's Jenny her hand the Truck in Boom Town Jenny's kiss used to be don't imagine nice bright honks from The Truck.

I THOUGHT IT WOULD BE FUNNY

I cut out a picture of a wheelbarrow and pasted it on to one side of a mother's day card I was making for Bubby, who had turned 81 and was recently discharged from the mental hospital. Underneath the wheelbarrow I printed the words

> BEFORE THEY CART YOU OFF TO YOUR GRAVE
> I JUST WANT TO WISH YOU...

I gave her the card at the Saigon Bistro where my family had gathered to celebrate. I watched her read the card. She muttered something, looking at no one, and turned it over, where the more conventional message

> HAPPY DIA DE MADRES

was printed, along with cut-out pictures of tropical fruit. She repeated the phrase *HAPPY DIA DE MADRES* and whispered *Oh that's nice*, stuffing the card back into the plastic bag containing her mother's day gift from me – a copy of Art Spiegelman's MAUS.

I asked her *Bubby, aren't you going to show your card to the family?* Smiling, her eyes cast at the table-cloth, Bubby said *No*. My mother took the card out of the plastic bag and read it, hate-clouds gathering on her face. Looking at me, she said

You're a horse's ass.

> In this way, I ruined
> mother's day.

OSTENTATION OF PEACOCKS *continued*

Perhaps there is a tale to be told still to be told I wonder what Ron Silliman will say about that will he say anything about that I've always wondered whether people think I'm hostile or whether I'm correct and it's them that are hostile I wish I could be happy living in the Bible Garden behind the Big Cathedral to be one of those two peacocks preening.

Have a cup of coffee it is an earthly delight spend forty minutes a day with pornography earthly delight kick some fuck in the face feel HEAP STRONG demand the deaths of your enemies wonder what it would be like if God in all His majesty was dressed in a peacock robe the eyespots of the peacock feathers His many eyed all seeing checks BEEF.

For the satanic dwarf K— E— must be spangled by a thousand bright lights and colors what distinguishes a color from a light what is the color black and what happens to it in the context of physics demand the deaths of your enemies if you must though the three great monotheistic religions preach love what's so a priori great about monotheism.

I wish beauty wasn't fleeting it's grating that it is even Hosanna's buttocks... I'm sorry to sound so typical well I am descending there is something about the peacock's feathers that suggests the possibility for eternal beauty which is I guess what I'm trying to get at here though let's face it I'm failing dismally Ponce De Leon went to Puerto Rico for it.

I'd rather be the troubadours than Dante Burns one of Shakes' Songs than any long poem built on a plan but them early natural days don't come no more this – that – it's there though I don't even bother to jot the things down any more after I get home it's not sterility I'm afraid of it's just there's as much juice here I think as in anybody or more.

– when you get super enthusiastic about things that we're talking about in class and when you leave us alone and tell us can I trust you talk about this I want to scream out Yes I will do anything you ask of me I long to do the love with you Kane O were I to be a finger in that pocket I know you probably wouldn't consentingly do the love with me –

This – that – it's there – right now – not a cow but a peacock – not an ocelot but an ostrich – the links between the two birds are I suspect intuitively manifold – she who bangs the door is chewing gum – she blows a terrible blast on her toy trumpet – which is right now happening – a flutter of wings – the wind – Lisa's weird camel face – Bart.

KAYAK TRIP

I went on a kayak trip   I succeeded at the kayak trip   I was in
    nature   I was OK.
I saw a heron   I befriended a heron   I paddled after it   it seemed
    to like me.

It waited for me   on an outcropping rock   as I paddled towards it
    it just hung around.
But when I got close to it   it flew to the next rock   where it
    waited for me   to play catch up again.

I paddled after it   heron acting like Lassie   the event was quiet
    and I communed.
I never thought   that I could commune   with a natural object   be
    it heron or tree

*   *

I wonder if anyone   would like to tell me   a little story about
    their kayak trip too.
For our force is quite fluid   chewing the kayak fat   cosmology
    radiant   a kind of mineral calm

For there are frogs   and there are tadpoles   there is fire   and
    there is a lake.
There is one river   hey here's another one   there is a beach   here
    a fat daisy.

Oh there is a twig   and there is an outhouse   sounding of giggle
    and there is some rot.
Now here is a ripple   and here is a plash   and there is scouring
    sand   oh and maybe a bulrush.

So there is a stone   and there is a kayak oar   there's a canoe   and
    then there is the sun.

A sun beam some bees lobelia some glass a pan and some
    bubbles leaf shade a slope

Oh come upward to sing with nostalgia o wings of a heron in
    clouds and the background for words
A bird glides some heron all feathers and shriek in the air of
    our surface whose name I'm not sure

Mix all sorts of scraps it's August my ears the orange has fallen
    night stinks of pine

I went on a kayak trip I succeeded at the kayak trip I was in
    nature I was OK.

OSTENTATION OF PEACOCKS *continued*

And me oh my my patterned shirt with flowers on it I am exotic I am delightful in my brightly patterned shirt it is this that I put on in the face of death this lovely flower patterned shirt this violet and pink and blue and green and white and flowered printed shirt the death tremors the shirt when the shirt is on less death tremors more confidence.

The circle of the lustful comforts me also stable patterns strings a long sustained note on the violin a long sustained and barely perceptible note on the French horn oh a long bird's neck the way it so often turns into a question mark most especially the swan a fine game bird in the olden days before becoming protected by our lovely Queen's royal decree.

Even dream of smooth integration into peafowl vagina creepy K— E— and we will know and you will be punished perhaps sent into woeful battle forever forbidden entrance into gorgeous Ding-Dong Valley you will also be trod upon first by an elephant and then by a whale at the judge's discretion you shall eternally trudge through darkness you fuck-wad.

Imagine wanting a penis instead of a vagina imagine lopping off your perfectly healthy breasts so you can appear more manly imagine attaching a fake penis to where your labia used to be imagine that it looks like a penis that's been run over by a truck now imagine someone loving you imagine waking up it's morning looking forward to evening's BEEF.

Malte Andersson please carry out some seminal research in the area of female choice please study long-tailed widow birds whose males have tails one and a half meters long and court by jumping in the air in the prairies where they live where they can be seen for a kilometer and a half Malte please cut some males' tails short down to 14 centimeters.

This morning I woke up ENGORGED with pleasure only to receive a phone call from The Snake letting me know my loved ones were being held hostage somewhere in the Docklands but don't even try to call the police or else they're all gonna get a bullet to the head so I did what I had to do I attached spurs to the claws of my peacock mounted guns.

Purple flowery red pink against blue an expectorant one hand washes the other oh what hairy grace today many colors crowds resenting America for all it has done to the peacocks and house bulbs my body heavy with artichoke pesto mad myself what grace in these here muscles and sinews sheet of flesh opening up shooting stars archery archery.

At dinner we chant we are fertile material equal in desire equal in rhyme we are against the West we assume that being easy and fun is enough for a day no more poignant than revolution are we all new all the time what we have in mind is a circle a bond a plethora of forms and constructions that fill us with frenzied joy as a bespattered city block.

OSTENTATION OF PEACOCKS *continued*

And by the way if you doubt that heaven is on earth then just go to the Bible Garden behind St. John the Divine and gaze upon the two peacocks that make their home there let your words get lost in the opus of peacock squeal and children's cries who study at the Cathedral School despite the churchy overtones no God just dumb born songs and light.

Square after square that are alive please elongate male birds' tails purple flowery red pink my cock popped blue out her mouth satiric and loose an urban night a harbor an art that is alive an iconoclastic impulse to produce night the wind whispers and repeats itself a car backs up stalls and backfires set and cut into shadow into night where is our supper.

First curse my enemies with this chant curse the treacherous J— P— of the thieving heart curse the satanic dwarf K— E— curse all who have failed to see the beauty of my manifold eyes my gorgeous gown my long spangled train curse them to the edge of the ocean curse them into the ocean the waves shall crash over their perfidious heads.

NOT A ROBOT am I but a small yellow pear a crab-apple a tiny lump of fat a tinker actually considerably taller than a wren and then I reach out to you oh my darling I shake my tail-feathers baby so alive am I so in love with buttocks and fish that my mother's very words 'Danny you will be a great lover' are sure to be made true shall be my legacy.

The Blue Apollo boy butterfly after fucking seals the genitalia of the girl with a sticky chemical the seal only breaks when her eggs are laid not a butterfly to fuck around with the peacock on the other hand acts like he's eating head to the ground the potential mate rushes over for a bite only to be seduced by his shining tail then everyone happily huphup.

Malte please elongate other male birds' tails please show that females do choose and what they want are males with long tails preferably artificially enhanced please observe a group of male peacocks and then clip the eye spots out of half the males' tails just the eye spots not the tail length please discover that females prefer males with the most eye spots.

This is what I fear that I am never invited to the things I should be invited to that I have become too old to be properly loved that they do not think it worth their while to love me though I am eminently loveable unlike the horrifying Blue Apollo boy butterfly if I was a little taller perhaps if I was bit more chilly and long but I appall so many I fall short.

I'd like to build myself more stately quarters than this but I just can't afford it I can't afford to have a variety of game birds deer and antelope wandering around this estate for the vile pleasure of some incestuous aristocrats I need more money than I get I am a very bitter gamekeeper no little Peter or Demeter to amuse me to blow me a wonderful blast.

I DID

I went ahead and got a cat. I named him
Kim Chi, because he suggested hot cabbage.

Fed him a mixture of wet and dry.
Cuddled him. Poked his belly etc.

Kim Chi will make my children kinder – people
who don't let in pets often issue bitter progeny.

I know this from some adults, the way
they don't jump around by the fruits and cakes.

It's about the mind, probably:
when a kid makes it out of the playpen,

he needs more than a thumb or breast. He needs
a little furry pack, something

that looks good running around a little
chair, a little table, oh little cat,

SECOND DATE WITH ESTHER DRILL

We were sitting close to each other in front of her computer, looking through the pages of an on-line magazine she had developed called 'GURL'. We scanned through a profile on Judy Blume. Then we read the rhapsody on cowgirls, heard snippets of Patti Smith, learned how to properly pop pimples.

Finally, Esther showed me the page displaying an illustration of the female reproductive system. Each part was highlighted – labia, fallopian tubes, vagina, clitoris, cervix. Esther

explained I should move the cursor to the part I wanted to learn about, then click. Once I clicked, the illustration would be replaced by a sub-page with detailed information on the part.

'Where do you want to go first'? she asked.

I moved the cursor over to the clitoris, and said quietly 'We may as well go here first'.

'Oh, good'. she said. 'That's my favorite part'.　　　　　clicked

The illustration disappeared, and the sub-page with clit-info came up. Esther and I read about how the clitoris, when rubbed or licked, may often result in a cum. As we read, the three sounds in Esther's room were　　　　the hum of her computer
our breathing　　　　　　　the occasional *honk honk* from outside

OSTENTATION OF PEACOCKS *continued*

What might it be like to dart tongue in Hosanna vagina what might it be like be tongued in asshole by little David what will it be like when I urinate on delightful Emily's face how do animals let us know something is theirs within a circle remember the orangutan in Manila how he used to bend over and piss on you succulent um uh warm arc.

Every day we wake up every day and a little stroke and squirt some pineapple perhaps a banana milkshake sea daisy so ambitious and the sky is well blue and the well wind and where does that wind come from does it rustle can you feel my fingers guiding the wind against your fair cheek can you feel the little hairs on my legs startle yours awake.

Tomoko had a party last night which I could not go to the party was with beans and rice the party oh so daubed whites blues blacks greens all suspicious all desiring all yes they preened and all pranced and all yes strutted yes and all wide mouths consuming capons wind against her window and uh people do that peacock strut uh huh.

People do that peacock strut uh huh using harsh and grating rimes like he goats rancorous they butt against each other their anger is uncontrolled they are hungry for the beef though we are not sure if they deserve the beef they trample on each others' feet and look how they move away from the catering hall despondent o blessed herald begot by Grace.

We eat cracked corn we eat wheat we eat snakes like candy we eat grasshoppers we eat cat-food grubs green grass we eat drunk wasps then we get drunk cricket sure we'll eat it we wouldn't mind some possum either we eat poison and thrive we eat leggy spiders crayfish lizards we eat beans we eat rice coyotes eat us we run away from danger.

In glorious Ding-Dong Valley there are no floods you'll be safe no evil coyotes no creepy-crawly K— E— you can walk along the forest-encrusted streets safe from fire and other ravages you can bake bread and sleep on mattresses stuffed with rosemary and your downtime can be spent with us wing-tip to wing-tip in circles throbbing with song.

AGAINST FUN

Drop, disappear for long stretches, lose your voice,
shimmer, shimmy and reflect using lots of artificial light,
play tricks with trap doors, sliding panels and false bottoms,

and generally have a terrific time. Return to the point of no return,
string a bunch of mirrors across the landscape,
stretch invisibly into the future, and don't forget

to generally have a terrific time. Poke a hole
into the canvas, slide the scale down to the shore,
legitimize perspective with the lure of subjectivity, and

generally have a terrific time

>even though everyone in the arena is pointing at you,
>doubled over with belly-laughs and other convulsions

>even though I'm very sad, my seeing-eye dog is dead,
>and everyone now willfully or witlessly serves
>>a horrible ideological function

OSTENTATION OF PEACOCKS *continued*

Tituba Tituba the girls are barking Tituba Tituba all guttural and witchy-like what the fuck is going on who's Tituba what's up with the chants the fear that's being aroused at the sight of our nice wholesome girls enchanted into some kind of demonic sexual ritual involving J— P— lederhosen and a kid named Martin oh save the intelligent girls.

Good love is purportedly all we need good loving baby but I have my doubts for example if I'm squeezed tight by my baby I don't always feel immediately better it is not the cure for my fever it is not all I really need even if you give me that loving I might not automatically think this world of ours terrific however if combined with roast game well.

I am Hercules struggling with Death and I am the beloved about to die I will hold a baby in my arms and not age even as that child dies I will remove stickers from products tattoos from bodies racial characteristics from faces I will remove the body from consideration and leave you like old days as pure spirit free of the hirsute body.

I speak to ask you to ply the bark with sail get the oars even if we're still indoors enjoying the meal for lo were I to stand and all respect forgo and ask B-i-n-g-o cuntface fucking assflaps to come on in well the lady in the manner of a lover might resume her singing and the demons would drop oiled clammy pitch upon us that would totally suck.

Are you enjoying the beef dinner I so lovingly prepared for you with your heart in mind vegetables and sauce and the presence of He Who is Most Holy the Royal Bird of Ages Most Divine do feel free to take more potatoes what you wish to caress me sure please touch me chiefly if it means your tongue my balls my thumb your mouth oh boy HUP.

But opening up mines and look I would say to this kindly being Hercules struggling with death it is true again more quietly and then time gallops time gallops withal I wonder if he knew that he was quoting Shakespeare the word surcharged or landslides I could have wished for him I could have made him look I would say through a secret door.

– but if you do I will cook you things like curry and samosas but they will have to be vegetable samosas as I am a vegetarian we can have apple pie for pudding if ever you need anything just put an X on your window that I can see and I will come with singular freshness and poignancy I will come with blinking hazards to bombard you with my love.

MUGOO

As a child, I gleefully accepted sexual advances
from Mugoo, my English sheep-dog. I would laugh,
squirming as I watched his penis slide out from its
hairy sheath, his front legs pinning my shoulders down.

When it came time to move from Mexico, we had to sell Mugoo –
heartbreak. He was the first thing outside my family
I remember loving.

Since then, I've become suspicious of everyone,
while in the past I'd walk up to strangers
just to talk about the day.

> Life was great with a friendly, sensual dog
> to play with on the green front-yard.

OSTENTATION OF PEACOCKS *continued*

Are you ready for discussion of the Absolute Beauty Absolute Truth Absolute Goodness the victorious mouth and don't forget the bird shining with its own lights emblazoned many-eyed near a box of oranges and a temporarily happy child her curled hair her skull insides intricate remind us a song sung as school-children sounds an echo.

A girl goes out for firewood and is taken by a bear to his cave where he offers her a feast of peacock he admits regret for not having an ostentation of peacocks on the grill but big peacock can feed small army the girl realizes she's left home she's encountered a problem she's um talking to um a *bear* there's another um really bad *congenital* problem.

Ginkgo leaf drifts light peacock green peacock and pheasant flowering tree ginkgo biloba buckbeans narcissus recently realized peacock blue base distance from ginkgo DNA sequence Japanese maple flowering kale maiden hair tree Yulan magnolia one part is grieving heart slays a peacock cornerstone beige peacock's proud colors probable root.

Mother and Father press loins against each other to this day indeed my mum's stated quite clearly that her favorite position's doggie style which interestingly enough is mine too Helena once said yeah doggie style is hot as I was like they say giving it to her doggie style how do peacocks mate is the expected question at this point do they do it doggie.

We used to have tails we know this and love it though we rarely discuss it the coccyx is still a vestigial reminder though so we can always tap it or something if we want to hark back to those fun times I wonder what my tail might have looked like probably nice and long monkey-like that's what my tail would've looked like yeah nice and monkey-like.

Moms busted a nut all over J— P— 's face for which we are grateful an ostentation of peacocks was brought out for the celebratory feast though the more conventional among us clamored for BEEF BEEF things like that the creepy K— E— thought he was invited but he wasn't oh the laughter at his chagrin we drowned him in a cute brooklet.

Who will turn into an animal me you who will hark our soft moist flesh when shall we hear the sirens sing again let alone the peacock's mournful squawk ought we to truly try and soar aloft if not why not never did nature or art convey such rapture to me as these creatures fair that reflect me in their many eyes I uplift mine eyes I strew red blossoms.

What wonders these what revelry of flashing rays no greater marvel is there than in thee unhindered shuffling around adorned madly in the basin of Ding-Dong Valley oh happy waddling friends all breathing crying the beauty which we see here I'm so happy I just want to pound away doggie-style to celebrate this our vast and happy sea of being.

To wake up a little and nibble on some pepperoni to receive tidings to press and slide and squeeze and snack on a tit or two to 'finger a wet teen slit' to break from the dance and stop in silence listening for a chord that radiates from Grace the very darling feeling for to dedicate my love with laughter to Her as the birds centre upon us like a chapel round.

As the birds centre upon us like a chapel round as they breathe as they beget as at these my words their desire ascends as I lead them from within the sun where I had entered into greater colors manifest to me I summon blazing eyes and pink violet blue green and white so sweet in the voice and bright the laughter ostentation of peacocks circling round.

POEM (*the sexiness of the ancient world*)

The sexiness of the ancient world
whether in cities still intact or now in ruins

is pretty hot, I admit it. But, come on,
compared to the miraculous pastel clarity of environment that
        the bells of the ice-cream truck engender

as their tinky peals mix with their lover the air as the truck wends
        its way east on 12th street,
then west on 13th and north on A, up to 14th street where it
        heads east again to make a right and go south

on B until 11th street, where it has to take an unexpected
right on 11th because of construction between 9th and 10th

streets on A?   Please, help this driver.
Even I do not know where he is now. It is like that song

about Poor Charlie who rode the streets of Boston,
the man who never returned   (The sound of ice-cream truck
        bells again out his window).

But wait, outside my window I hear the bells again, and
the barking of a medium-sized dog. It is OK, I suppose. It sounds

like the truck's heading east again, maybe on 10th. Perhaps
it will go north on C and west on 11th three blocks to A, north
        one block then east again on 12th, where

I can run out of the building and flag the ice-cream truck down,
buy a Supersicle Sour Tower, a Choco Taco, a Twister Cool Blue.

CHOCO-TACO CREAMY BURGER TINGLY CENTERS

Farm boys eating ice-cream cones   Washington, Indiana
Children hand-cranking ice cream   Caswell County, North Carolina

Pie-crust cones flecked with cherry bits   Crowley, Louisiana
Oh the children do cry unable to choose   in Phillipsburg, Montana

Indestructo and Heart Disher   just some of our ice-cream scoopers
"My first round bowl dipper was like a friend"   says Mom as she
    rounds the bend

One's shaped like a cow and "mooooooooos"   one even cries out
    "Ice Cream!"
Just some of the sounding dippers   dreamed up by one Wayne Smith

13% of men admit   to licking the bowl when they're done
only 8% of women say   they do that when they're done

Nearly 5% of ice-cream eaters   share with their dogs or cats
About 7% who sit in ball-field bleachers   are seen lapping at the stuff

It's chocolate ice cream, squash bugs, and friends   in the center and
    our coasts
Guzzle oh Conway, Mattapan   your own place you choose wherever

Pump ice cream out of anyone's basement   and things are bound
    to improve
Hand out cones beyond states and kingdoms   cones in our hands
    are wands

OSTENTATION OF PEACOCKS *concluded*

How did the peacock get his tail this question has tormented zoologists for more than a century the wind is currently rustling the leaves of the gingko tree and outside in the square is a playground with a toddler-sized swing set climbing jungle and slide if we close our eyes really tightly and wait the whole universe Ding-Dong Valley moving.

These works first appeared in the following journals; 'A Dairy Maid in the Act of Teasing a Cow that Wishes to be a Dairy Maid,' *Pavement Saw Press*; 'Beginning with Flapping' and 'Kayak Trip,' *Tarpaulin Sky*; 'Fish 1/Fish 2,' *Lit*; 'Poem (The Sexiness of the Ancient World)' and 'Absenteeism in the Work Place,' *Painted Bride Quarterly*; 'Choco Taco,' *nthposition*; 'Little Goat Song,' *The Spook*; 'Ambivalent Picnic' and 'Sonnet: Dear Fire,' *Jacket*; 'Invitation' and 'Against Fun,' *The Hat*; 'Variations and The Whole Darn Lot of Us,' *Fence*; 'Sonnet,' *Skanky Possum*; 'Jewish Variations on Erik Satie's 'Sports et Divertissements',' *TriQuarterly*; 'Hostile Stuff,' *Hanging Loose*; 'I Thought it Would Be Funny,' *Exquisite Corpse*.

'Ostentation of Peacocks' appeared as a single poem in *Jacket*.

The poems in Part 2 of this book were previously collected and published in the chapbook *SEVEN* (Landfill Press, 2005), and in *Fence* (2005).

The line "I'm really lost hopelessly immersed in lyric" is borrowed from David Trinidad's poem 'Sometimes it seems the Night Conspires'.